FOR THE CHILDREN

A Collection of Poems and Stories for Children of all ages

Compiled by Marilyn Rose

PRINTWISE PUBLICATIONS LIMITED

Published by Printwise Publication Ltd
47 Bradshaw Road, Tottington, Bury, Lancs, BL8 3PW.

Warehouse and Orders
40-42 Willan Industrial Estate, Vere Street,
Salford, M5 2GR.
Tel: 061-745 9168 Fax: 061-737 1755

Production co-ordinated by

Cliff Hayes

ISBN No. 1 872226 14 0

Printed and bound by Manchester Free Press,
Paragon Mill, Jersey Street,
Manchester, M4 6FP. Tel: 061-236 8822.

Introduction

On Friday May 29th 1987 Marilyn and Brian Rose were devastated to find out that their only son David was dying...he was only 11 months old. It is impossible to imagine the horror of learning that their beautiful son was suffering from the rare genetic disease "Tay Sachs". Three years later David died.

Marilyn courageously decided to try and prevent this tragedy from affecting other families and become deeply involved in publicising the effects of the disease and how it could be avoided; she also helped organise various fund-raising events. The many and varied activities, as well as looking after his 3 older sisters, kept her fully occupied - and helped her to deal with day-to-day trauma of coping with David.

One of Marilyn's projects was to compile materials for a children's book: she wrote, badgered and chased the famous and talented to contribute to this book. Not only will sales raise desperately-needed funds but it will leave David's name connected forever with a book of love and hope, to please and amuse the children of today, and hopefully the many children who will read it in the years to come.

Marilyn has put together one of the best collections of children's verse and stories - one to be treasured for many, many features.

The celebrities and writers responded magnificently and after a lot of chasing, cajoling, and correspondence, Marilyn ended up with this unique collection. She needed a publisher, and after a few disappointments we heard her appeal on the radio and said that we would look into the project. I do not use the word lightly when I say that we (Andrew, Dawn, Sylvia and myself) at Printwise Publications are honoured to join in with this venture.

CLIFF HAYES

Acknowledgements

There were times over the last five years when it looked like this book would never see the light of day, so extra special hugs are due to Suzie Mathis, Sandra Shapiro and Carolyn Dinan. Suzie featured us on her programme and found us Cliff our very own publisher; Sandra and Carolyn sketched many of the beautiful drawings that brighten up this book.

Without Sandra & Carolyn — dull book

Without Suzie — no publisher.

Without Cliff — no book!

Nuff said.

If you would like to know more, or help further,
Please contact...

"David Rose Tay Sachs Fund"
affiliated to "Tay-Sachs and Allied Diseases Association"
Charity Commission Registration No. 326403
c/o 130, Church Street, Eccles, M30 OLS
Tel: 061 - 789 3207

The proceeds from this book will go directly to the David Rose Tay Sachs Fund and from there will be split between the Manchester Children's Hospital and the Tay Sachs Association. All the money raised will stay in the area and be used for helping others.

About Tay Sachs

Tay Sachs is an inherited disorder caused by the absence of a vital enzyme resulting in the destruction of the nervous system. One in twenty five Jewish people carry the faulty enzyme , but it is not just a problem for the Jewish community. One in 250 non-Jewish people are carriers, and 15% of the babies who died last year were non-Jewish.

It is always fatal; and to date there is no known cure. No one has ever survived once it has been diagnosed.

A Tay Sachs baby develops normally for the first few months. Then a relentless deterioration of mental and physical abilities begins. Blindness creeps over the child, paralysis begins and then unable to swallow the child slips away from the world, and eventually loses contact with the loved ones around them.

Dedications

For David with Love

This book is dedicated to our son David who died aged 3 years 11 months from Tay Sachs disease - a rare genetic disorder which is fatal. The money raised from the sale of this book will go to help provide funds for screening, and the continuing search for a cure.

Contents

Contents

My Little Boy *Brian Rose*

My little boy
Went out to school today
Trailed his satchel on the ground
In a schoolboy sort of way
He ran and shouted in the yard
The schoolbell he ignored
The English, French and History
Had clearly left him bored
He kicked a football round at lunch
The goals he scored were go
But ducking past a full-back's punch
He slipped into some mud
He came home late and tired
Another happy day
He ate and drank the buns and squash
He didn't have much to say
In fact he never says much
In fact I wish he would
In fact this never happened
In fact I wish it could.

Brian Rose

The Magic Recorder *Thelma Lambert*

Once upon a time, not that long ago, last week in fact, there was a little girl called Lizzie. She had long brown plaits and a big smile which had a gap where she'd lost her front teeth. She lived with her Mum and two dogs called Jack and Jill. But the main thing you ought to know about Lizzie was this: she was always losing things.

She lost her watch the week after her birthday; she lost her nice new costume at the swimming pool; she lost a ballet shoe at her very first class. And as for her dinner money, she lost *that* at least once a week. Sometimes twice.

Well now, it was coming up for Christmas and everyone at Lizzie's school was very excited because they were going to do a play. Lizzie had been chosen to be an angel. She was pleased because it meant you got to wear a long frock, wings and tinsel in your hair.

Rehearsals began in earnest. The children made waves with blue cloth and three cardboard ships came bobbing along the back of the stage. And the angels played "I Saw Three Ships Come Sailing In' on their recorders.

Lizzie would practise her recorder whenever she could: on the bus, at the tea-table, once even in the bath.

Well. Of course it had to happen, didn't it? Lizzie lost her recorder.

"Oh LIZZIE! Not your recorder!" sighed Mr Lewis. He seemed pretty mad. But the next morning her teacher came smiling into the class carrying a black box.

"It's my Grandmother's recorder! he said. "And if you *promise* not to lose it, Lizzie, you can borrow it for tomorrow!"

Lizzie gave a big grin, showing all her gap. She couldn't wait to practise her tune - she was worried she might have forgotten it - she hadn't played it for two whole days it was an old wooden recorder, not a bit like the plastic ones everyone else had. Lizzie stroked the

The entire audience began to dance

pale wood with her finger. Then she began to play: and to everyone's amazement Mr Lewis began to DANCE! He flung up his arms, he kicked his heels as he twirled round the room! The children stamped their feet in time with the music.

Just then Miss Phillip, the headmistress, came bursting in.

"What on EARTH—!" But before she could finish the sentence she too began to dance! Tall, dignified, hardly-ever-smiling Miss Phillip! Her glasses slipped down her nose and the dust flew under her feet as she stamped and kicked.

Then Lizzie suddenly stopped playing; and at once the two grown ups stopped dancing. Mr Lewis sat down and began to take the register as if nothing had happened. Miss Phillip smoothed her hair and tottered out of the room, quite forgetting what she'd come about.

After that Lizzie played the recorder whenever she wanted to make someone dance; but it only worked on grown-ups. She played it on the bus and the conductor was so busy dancing he forgot to ask for their fares. Lizzie played it when Mr Wilkins came round to complain about Jack and Jill digging up his lawn; he danced so energetically he quite forgot what he had come about!

Lizzie played her recorder for the milkman in the morning: he danced down the street delivering the milk! He looked like one of those T.V. commercials.

And in the afternoon it was the school play. Time to put on net frock, wings and tinsel. Time to play the magic recorder...

The hall was packed with mums and dads and grannies, even the dinner ladies had squeezed in at the back.

Class One began making waves with the blue cloth and the three ships began to wobble across the stage. The angels began to play their recorders and Lizzie's was the loudest of all:

"I Saw Three Ships Come Sailing In, Come Sailing In..."

The entire audience rose to its feet and began to - DANCE!

The old grannies with their bad knees, the stout dinner ladies, the mums and aunts and teachers! And as far as I know, they are dancing still!

Thelma Lambert

The Whatsit

Tony Bradman

I think I've lost my whatsit,
the one I got last year
For Christmas, or my birthday . . .
It's simply disappeared.

I had it just the other day,
I put it on the floor;
Or was it in the thingummybob?
The one behind the door?

I got it from old what's-his-name,
Or was it from his brother?
It's blue, I think, or maybe red.
There couldn't be another.

I'm sure I left it somewhere,
Perhaps it's in the hall . . .
But now I come to think of it,
It can't be there at all.

I'll have to keep on looking,
I know it's somewhere near . .

How can my favourite whatsit
Have simply disappeared?

Tony Bradman

Sally Won't You Walk with Me?

Gareth Owen

"Sally won't you walk with me
Walking heel and toe
Sally can we secrets share
As home from school we go."

Arm in arm by lane and hedge
So many tales to tell
And every tale breeds tales anew
As we walk in a magic spell.

And do you know what Brenda said
And how Alan banged his head
How Antonia cried at dinner time
And what Jemima said?"

"And wasn't dinner awful?
And Sally tell your dream
And will you come to tea next week?
And isn't Rose a scream?"

"Did you really tell your mother that
Did your sister cut your hair
Did you see that lady on the bike
Did you see those two boys stare?"

"And Sally, look, stop giggling
Oh Sally honestly
Oh Sally don't you pull that face
Those people there will see."

"What did your father say to that
And did you do it again?
You didn't really, I don't believe!
Sally what happened then?"

We whisper over Sally's gate
Till her mother calls her to tea
So many secrets still to tell
So many tales about me.

If I could wish my days again
If time were a golden spool
I'd wish I could walk for ever
With Sally home from school.

The Balaclava Story *George Layton*

Tony and Barry both had one. I reckon half the kids in our class had one. But I didn't. My mum wouldn't even listen to me.

"You're not having a balaclava! What do you want a balaclava for in the middle of summer?"

I must've told her about ten times why I wanted a balaclava.

"I want one so's I can join the Balaclava Boys..."

"Go and wash your hands for tea, and don't be silly."

She turned away from me to lay the table, so I put the curse of the middle finger on her. This was pointing both your middle fingers at somebody when they weren't looking. Tony had started it when Miss Taylor gave him a hundred lines for flicking paper pellets at Jennifer Greenwood. He had to write out a hundred times: "I must not fire missiles because it is dangerous and liable to cause damage to someone's eye."

Tony tried to tell Miss Taylor that he hadn't fired a missile, he'd just flicked a paper pellet, but she threw a piece of chalk at him and told him to shut up.

"Don't just stand there - wash your hands."

"Eh?"

"Don't say "eh', say "pardon'."

"What?"

"Just hurry up, and make sure the dirt comes off in the water, and not on the towel, do you hear?"

Ooh, my mum. She didn't half go on sometimes.

"I don't know what you get up to at school. How do you get so dirty?"

I knew exactly the kind of balaclava I wanted. One just like Tony's, a sort of yellowy-brown. His dad had given it to him because of his earache. Mind you, he didn't like wearing it at first. At school he's given it to Barry to wear and got it back before home-time. But, all the other lads started asking if they could have a wear of it, so Tony took it back and said from then on nobody but him could wear it, not even Barry. Barry told him he wasn't bothered because he was going to get a balaclava of his own, and so did some of the other lads. And that's how it started - the Balaclava Boys.

It wasn't a gang really. I mean they didn't have meetings or anything like that. They just went around together wearing their balaclavas, and if you didn't have one you couldn't go around with them. Tony and Barry were my best friends, but because I didn't have a balaclava, they wouldn't let me go around with them. I tried.

"Aw, go on, Barry, let us walk round with you."

"No, you can't. You're not a Balaclava Boy."

"Aw, go on."

"No."

"Please."

I don't know why I wanted to walk round with them anyway. All they did was wander up and down the playground dressed in their rotten balaclavas. It was daft.

"Go on, Barry, be a sport."

"I've told you. You're not a Balaclava Boy. You've got to have a balaclava. If you get one, you can join."

"But I can't, Barry. My mum won't let me have one."

"Hard luck."

"You're rotten."

Then he went off with the others. I wasn't half fed up. All my friends were in the Balaclava Boys. All the lads in my class except me. Wasn't fair. The bell went for the next lesson - ooh heck, handicraft with the Miseryguts Garnett - then it was home-time. All the Balaclava Boys were going in and I followed them.

"Hey, Tony, do you want to go down the woods after school?"

"No, I'm going round with the Balaclava Boys."

"Oh."

Blooming Balaclava Boys. Why wouldn't my mum buy me a balaclava? Didn't she realise that I was losing all my friends, and just because she wouldn't buy me one?

"Eh, Tony, we can go goose-gogging - you know, by those great gooseberry bushes at the other end of the woods."

"I've told you, I can't."

"Yes, I know, but I thought you might want to go goose-gogging."

"Well, I would, but I can't."

I wondered if Barry would be going as well.

"Is Barry going round with the Balaclava Boys an' all?"

"Course he is."

"Oh."

Blooming balaclavas. I wish they'd never been invented.

"Why won't your mum get you one?"

"I don't know. She says it's daft wearing a balaclava in the middle of summer. She won't let me have one."

"I found mine at home up in our attic."

Tony unwrapped some chewing-gum and asked me if I wanted a piece.

"No thanks." I'd've only had to wrap it in my handkerchief once we got in the classroom. You couldn't get away with anything with Mr. Garnett.

"Hey, maybe you could find one in your attic." For a minute I wasn't sure what he was talking about.

"Find what?"

"A balaclava."

"No, we haven't even got an attic."

I didn't half find handicraft boring. All that mucking bout with compasses and rulers. Or else it was weaving, and you got all tangled up with balls of wool. I was just no good at handicraft and Mr. Garnett agreed with me. Today was worse than ever. We were painting pictures and we had to call it "My favourite story." Tony was painting "Noddy in Toyland." I told him he'd get into trouble.

"Garnett'll do you."

"Why? It's my favourite story."

"Yes, but I don't think he'll believe you."

Tony looked ever so hurt.

"But honest. It's my favourite story. Anyway, what are you doing?"

He leaned over to have a look at my favourite story.

"Have you read it, Tony?"

"I don't know. What is it?"

"It's Robinson Crusoe', what do you think it is?" He just looked at my painting.

"Oh, I see it now. Oh yes, I get it now. I couldn't make it out for a minute. Oh yes, there's Man Friday behind him."

"Get your finger off, it' still wet. And that isn't Man Friday, it's a coconut tree. And you've smudged it."

We were using some stuff called poster paint, and I got covered in it. I was getting it everywhere, so I asked Mr Garnett if I could go for a wash. He gets annoyed when you ask to be excused, but he could see I'd got it all over my hands, so he said I could go, but told me to be quick.

The washbasins were in the boy's cloakroom just outside the main hall. I got most of the paint off and as I was drying my hands, that's when it happened. I don't know what came over me. As soon as I saw that balaclava lying on the floor, I decided to pinch it. I couldn't help it. I just knew that this was my only chance. I've never pinched anything before - I don't think I have - but I didn't think of this as ... well ... I don't even like saying it, but ... well stealing. I just did it.

I picked it up, went to my coat, and put it in the pocket but it bulged

They just went round together wearing their balaclavas

out, so I pushed it down the inside of the sleeve. My head was throbbing, and even though I'd just dried my hands, they were all wet from sweating. If only I'd thought a bit first. But it all happened so quickly. I went back to the classroom, and as I was going in I began to realise what I'd done. I'd stolen a balaclava. I didn't even know whose it was, but as I stood in the doorway I couldn't believe I'd done it. If only I could go back. In fact I thought I would but then Mr Garnett told me to hurry up and sit down. As I was going back to my desk I felt as if all the lads knew what I'd done. How could they? Maybe somebody had seen me. No! Yes! How could they? They could. Of course they couldn't. No, course not. What if they did though? Oh heck.

I thought home-time would never come but when the bell did ring I got out as quickly as I could. I was going to put the balaclava back before anybody noticed; but as I got to the cloakroom I heard Norbert Lighttowler shout out that someone had pinched his balaclava. Nobody took much notice, thank goodness, and I heard Tony say to him that he's most likely lost it. Norbert said he hadn't but he went off to make sure it wasn't in the classroom.

I tried to be casual and took my coat, but I didn't dare put it on in case the balaclava popped out of the sleeve. I said tarah to Tony.

"Tarah, Tony, see you tomorrow."

"Yeh, tarah."

Oh it was good to get out in the open air. I couldn't wait to get home and get rid of that blooming balaclava. Why had I gone and done a stupid thing like that? Norbert Lighttowler was sure to report it to the Headmaster, and there'd be an announcement about it as assembly and the culprit would be asked to own up. I was running home as fast as I could. I wanted to stop and take out the balaclava an chuck it away, but I didn't dare. The faster I ran, the faster my head was filled with thoughts. I could give it back to Norbert. You know, say I'd taken it by mistake. No, he'd never believe me. None of the lads would believe me. Everybody knew how much I wanted to be a Balaclava Boy. I'd have to get rid of the blooming thing as fast as I could.

My mum wasn't back from work when I got home, thank goodness, so as soon as I shut the front door, I put my hand down the sleeve of my coat for the balaclava. There was nothing there. That was funny, I was sure I'd put it down that sleeve. I tried down the other sleeve, and there was still nothing there. Maybe I'd got the wrong coat. No, it was my coat all right. Oh, blimey, I must've lost it while I was running home. I was glad in a way. I was going to have to get rid of it, now it was gone. I only hoped nobody had seen it drop out, but, oh, I was glad to be rid of it. Mind you, I was dreading going to school next morning. Norbert'd've probably have reported it by now. Well, I wasn't going to own up. I didn't mind the cane, it wasn't that, but if you owned up, you had to go up on the stage in front of the whole school. Well I was going to forget about it now and nobody would ever know that I'd pinched that blooming lousy balaclava.

I started to do my homework, but I couldn't concentrate. I kept thinking about assembly next morning. What if I went all red and everybody else noticed? They'd know I'd pinched it then. I tried to think about other things, nice things. I thought about bed. I just wanted to go to sleep. To go to bed and sleep. Then I thought about my mum; what she'd say if she knew I'd been stealing. But I still couldn't forget about assembly next day. I went into the kitchen and peeled some potatoes for my mum. She was ever so pleased when she came in from work and said I must've known she'd brought me a present.

"Oh, thanks. What've you got me?"

She gave me a paper bag and when I opened it I couldn't believe my eyes - a blooming balaclava.

"There you are, now you won't be left out and you can stop making my life a misery."

"Thanks, Mum."

If only my mum knew she was making my life a misery. The balaclava she'd brought me was just like the one I'd pinched. I felt sick. I didn't want it. I couldn't wear it now. If I did, everybody would say it was Norbert Lightowler's. Even if they didn't, I just couldn't wear it. I wouldn't feel it was mine. I had to get rid of it. I went outside and put it down the lavatory. I had to pull the chain three times before it went away. It's a good job we've got an outside lavatory or else my mum would have wondered what was wrong with me.

I could hardly eat my tea.
"What's wrong with you? Aren't you hungry?"
"No, not much."
"Don't you feel well?"
"I'm all right."
I wasn't, I felt terrible. I told my mum I was going upstairs to work on my model aeroplane.
"Well, it's my bingo night, so make yourself some cocoa before you go to bed."
I went upstairs to bed, and after a while I fell asleep. The last thing I remember was a big balaclava, with a smiling face, and it was the Headmaster's face.
I was scared stiff when I went to school next morning. In assembly it seemed different. All the boys were looking at me. Norbert Lightowler pushed past and didn't say anything. When prayers

"I could hardly eat my tea." "What's wrong with you? Aren't you hungry?".

finished I just stood there waiting for the Headmaster to ask for the culprit to own up, but he was talking about the school fete. And then he said he had something very important to announce and I could feel myself going red. My ears were burning like anything and I was going hot and cold both at the same time.

"I'm very pleased to announce that the school football team has won the inter-league cup..."

And that was the end of assembly, except that we were told to go and play in the schoolyard until we were called in, because there was a teacher's meeting. I couldn't understand why I hadn't been found out yet, but I still didn't feel any better, I'd probably be called to the Headmaster's room later on.

I went out into the yard. Everybody was happy because we were having extra playtime. I could see all the Balaclava Boys going round together. Then I saw Norbert Lightowler was one of them. I couldn't be sure it was Norbert because he had a balaclava on, so I had to go up close to him. Yes, it was Norbert. He must have bought a new balaclava that morning.

"Have you bought a new one, then, Norbert?"

"Y'what?"

"You've bought a new balaclava, have you?"

"What are you talking about?"

"Your balaclava. You've got a new balaclava, haven't you?"

"No, I never lost it, at all. Some fool had shoved it down the sleeve of my raincoat."

George Layton

Sick

Shel Silverstein

"I cannot go to school today."
Said little Peggy Ann McKay.
"I have the measles and the mumps,
A gash, a rash and purple bumps.
My mouth is wet, my throat is dry,
My tonsils are as big as rocks,
I've counted sixteen chicken pox
And there's one more – that's seventeen,
And don't you think my face looks green?
My leg is cut, my eyes are blue -
It might be instamatic flu,
I cough and sneeze and gasp and choke,
I'm sure that my left leg is broke -
My belly button's caving in,
My back is wrenched, my ankle's sprained,
My "pendix pains each time it rains.
My nose is cold, my toes are numb,
I have a sliver in my thumb.
My neck is still, my spine is weak,
I hardly whisper when I speak.
My tongue is filling up my mouth,
I think my hair is falling out.
My elbow's bent, my spine ain't straight,
My temperature is one-o-eight.

My brain is shrunk, I cannot hear,
There is a hole inside my ear.
I have a hangnail, and my heart is – what?
What's that? What's that you say?
You say today is ... Saturday?
G'bye, I'm going out to play!''

Shel Silverstein

A Million Beer Can Rings

Catherine Storr

Jamie had been told that a million of the metal beer can rings that you see littered about on every pavement, would be worth enough money to buy a kidney machine.

Jamie's twin brother, Fred, had been in a bad accident and since then his kidneys hadn't worked properly. Three times a week he had to travel fifteen miles for dialysis and the rest of the time he usually didn't feel well. That was why Jamie started collecting.

The first day he got eight rings. The second day he got eleven. At the end of the week, he counted his finds and he had fifty three.

When he'd got eight hundred and ninety-three he began to wonder if he'd ever get as many as a million. A thousand times a thousand, and he hadn't got one thousand yet. It was summer and searching in the dust for the rings was hot, boring work. At this rate, it would be years before he'd collected a million. And Fred was miserable. He often looked at Jamie, healthy and good a sport and doing all the things Fred'd have liked to and said, "It isn't fair!"

It wasn't fair. Jamie agreed with Fred about this.

At first, his friends had been quite keen to help. They had brought him rings they'd collected. They'd kept on asking, "Have you got a million yet?" But it wasn't long before they got tired of walking slowly, with their eyes turned down so that they could spot the odd ring. Gradually, one by one, they stopped searching, and when Jamie's collection had reached four thousand and one, only Fiona was helping, and she didn't bring in much. She was only four.

Jamie began to despair.

It was because he was looking for the can rings that he had his accident. He was in one of the best places, a lay-by on a double carriage-way, when a couple of cars drove in, very fast. The driver of the one in front swerved in order to avoid the second which was coming up too close. Jamie got knocked down. He wasn't badly hurt, but he had a gash on one leg which wouldn't stop bleeding. He had to be taken to hospital to have it sewn up.

While the doctor was stitching (with a local anaesthetic so it didn't hurt) Jamie asked her, "Do you have kidney machines here?"

"We do."

"How much do they cost?"

"Very expensive. Thousands of pounds. Why?"

Jamie told her about the beer can rings, and how he didn't think he was ever going to manage to collect a million.

"I'm afraid that's just a story. Even if you did manage to get that many, you wouldn't get nearly enough money for a kidney machine."

Jamie felt miserable. All that work for nothing!

"Did I hurt you? Sorry!" the doctor said.

"It wasn't that. It's Fred. My twin." And he told her about Fred's rotten kidneys and how he couldn't play games or do anything ordinary.

"Are you identical twins?" the doctor asked, carefully putting in the last stitch.

"Mm. We used to look so like each other no one could tell us apart. But now he's ill, we're different,' Jamie said.

"You know what? You might be able to give him one of your kidneys,' the doctor said.

"Wouldn't I miss it?"

"Not if both yours are healthy. But we'd have to do tests on you and Fred, and your parents would have to agree. And you ought to think about it seriously. There's a certain amount of risk,' the doctor said, putting away the needle.

Fred wasn't sure about it. Jamie's mother and father weren't sure. But in the end, Jamie persuaded them. "After all, he's my twin. If we'd been one boy, we'd only have had two kidneys. It's fair he should have one of mine,' he said.

"It's a lot better than a kidney machine,' Fred said, coming back from a football game.

"It's a lot quicker than trying to collect a million beer can rings,' Jamie agreed.

Catherine Storr.

It's My Kick Next

Michael Hardcastle

Peter Calvert was furious with his team-mates. They were still refusing to let him take a penalty kick. their team, Rangers, had been winning games by huge margins. Yet Peter was the only one who hadn't scored a goal all season. He thought it was about time he was given a chance to show what he could do.

There was, however, one problem: Peter was the team's goal-keeper. And goalkeepers, as the skipper kept pointing out, didn't take penalty kicks. In vain, Peter insisted that some goalies did; he'd heard of it once happening in a First Division match. But, no, he couldn't remember which match that was.

In desperation, he told Jimmy, the captain, what he would do if he wasn't given the next kick: he would go on strike. He would flatly refuse to stay between his posts. Peter was not only a splendid keeper: he was Rangers' only keeper.

So Jimmy had to give in. Reluctantly, he promised that Peter should take Rangers' next penalty. Peter was ecstatic at the thought of at last getting his name on the score-sheet.

As things turned out, the team weren't awarded a penalty in any of their next four League matches. They won three, drew one and went to the top of the league. Peter, too, was in good form and conceded only two goals in the four games – and one of those was the result of an appalling error by a Rangers full-back.

Then, in a Cup semi-final, with Rangers leading 1-0 against the Colts, Jimmy was brought down in the box. He was about to take the penalty kick himself when Peter reached the spot after rushing the length of the field to remind him of his promise. "It's my turn, you said so,' Rangers' goalkeeper declared forcefully, putting his foot on the ball at the same time.

Jimmy was a truthful boy who kept his word. So, reluctantly again, he stood aside, fingers crossed, as Peter lined up his kick. Peter had practised hard for weeks and his recent average had been eight successes out of ten. He took a long run at the ball, struck it well – but unhappily sent it straight into the arms of the Colts' goalkeeper who held on to it thankfully.

While Peter and Jimmy just groaned with disappointment the Colts' goalie reacted quickly and booted the ball as far as he could upfield. It was collected by a team-mate who passed to another player....and next moment, with Rangers' goal-mouth unguarded, a defender had to fist the ball over the bar to prevent a certain goal.

Peter was still racing back to his post when the referee pointed to the penalty spot. But, fortunately, he was allowed time to settle down before he faced the kick. Jimmy went up for a word with him.

"Best of luck, Peter,' was what he said. Not a word about the kick Peter himself had missed.

The Colts' penalty-taker hit the ball with all his strength, aiming for a spot just inside the post. Peter, though, had seen the direction in which the kicker had glanced before shooting. He judged his dive superbly and stopped the ball right on the line.

"Oh, great save, Peter, great save!" Jimmy enthused. "You see, that's what we need you for – to prevent goals, not score "em. Stopping a goal is just as important as scoring one."

Peter didn't disagree. For the rest of the match he kept his goal intact and so Rangers won 1-0 to reach the Cup Final.

All the same, in the moments when he wasn't very busy Peter Calvert thought very carefully about how to make certain of scoring when he took his next penalty kick....

Hello, I'm Home! *June Crebbin*

I'm not dirty –

My track suit's not dirty either
Because I took it off,
Even though it was cold.

I'm taking off my boots now.
They're dirty, of course,
But I'm taking them off out here.

I'll be in in a minute.
I didn't fall over once.
I'm not dirty –

Look. Look at me,
I'm not dirty, am I?

I don't need a bath.

Why do I need a bath
When I'm not dirty?
I played a clean game.

I'm going, I'm going –

BUT I'M NOT DIRTY ...

June Crebbin

Lies *Kit Wright*

When we are bored
My friend and I
Tell
Lies
It's a competition: the prize
Is won by the one
Whose lies
Are the bigger size.
We really do.
That's true
But there isn't a prize:
That's lies.

Kit Wright

Skipper and Sam and the Lovely Surprise for Mum

Carolyn Dinan

"I'm going to decorate the kitchen" said Mum, "We'll have to shut Skipper Dog out till it's finished."

"I'll help,' said Sam. "I'm good at painting."

"You can spread out the newspapers so I don't make a mess on the floor. Would you do that?" asked Mum. "I just have to pop upstairs for half-an-hour to help Sarah with her homework."

Sam waited till Mum had gone and then looked at the pile of newspapers. Then he looked at the paint. There was no doubt which was more interesting. He prised the top off the paint with a spoon-handle, put the sticky lid face upwards on the floor, peering inside the tin. The paint was like a thick cream jelly. Sam picked up a big fluffy roller and rolled it along the shiny paint-tray.

"I know just what to do," he thought, "It's easy. I'm going to give Mum a lovely surprise."

Skipper sniffed at the paint and sat down by the tin. He watched as Sam carefully scooped some into the tray and rolled it about till the roller was thickly covered.

"Out of my way, Skipper," said Sam, "Here goes!"

Skipper watched in astonishment as the wall began to

Skipper watched in astonishment as the wall began to change colour

change colour. Sam seemed to be changing colour too as the white paint spattered over his hair and dungarees. Then a blob of paint landed on Skipper's nose and he leaped back in alarm.

"Clang, bang, clatter!" Skipper nearly jumped out of his skin with fright. "Clatter, CLANGGGBANGG!" Something heavy was clinging to his tail, something that clashed and crashed as he bolted wildly round the kitchen.

"Skipper!" roared Sam, "Stop! You've sat on the paint-lid."

Skipper wasn't listening. He lay on his back and pushed at the lid with his paws. Then he tried to bite it but it tasted very nasty indeed and he swallowed rather a lot of paint by mistake. At last with a frantic flick of his tail he managed to send the lid spinning across the room.

"If you'd just keep still for one minute I could clean you up," wailed Sam, but Skipper couldn't keep still. He was much too

Something heavy was clinging to his tail ...

pleased at having got rid of that horrible noisy Thing on his tail. He jumped all over Sam, leaving white pawprints on his denim dungarees and wagged his tail happily against the clean blue tablecloth. He felt much better and if he could just get rid of the nasty taste of paint in his mouth he would feel better still . . .

"Oh no," groaned Sam, "Skipper, please don't be sick. Not on the rug."

But it was too late.

Sam mopped at the rug with a dirty rag but he seemed to be making it worse. The kitchen didn't look how he had meant it to look at all. There were white pawprints and splashes of paint all across the patterned floor and smears of paint on all the furniture. Sam gazed down at the roller in his hand and watched it drip paint on his shoes. He had had enough. Decorating was definitely not as simple as he had thought.

At that moment Sarah put her head round the door. "I've done my homework," she said, "Now we can start painting the...oh Sam! What will Mum say?"

Mum said a great deal. Skipper sighed heavily and slunk to his basket. He curled himself up inside, propped his chin on the rim, and rolled his eyes sadly at Sam. He didn't like when Mum raised her voice.

"It wasn't Skipper's fault," said Sam, "He got an awful fright. Don't worry, Mum, I'll soon have it cleared up."

Mum shuddered, "We'll do it together," she said firmly.

A few days later Granny came to tea.

"Your kitchen looks beautiful," she exclaimed. "You must have worked very hard decorating it."

Mum smiled at Sam, and at Skipper dozing peacefully on the newly washed rug.

"We certainly did," she said.

Carolyn Dinan

He had had enough.

The Rescue

June Counsel

William was putting hats on snails. They were his snails, that is they lived in his garden, and they all had names. He picked up a red ribbed bottle top with a little lip sticking out and stuck it on top of the largest snail's shell with sellotape.

"There, Grandfather,' he said. "There's a military hat for you."

Grandfather stared about him importantly like a general inspecting his troops. The sun rose higher. The dew began to dry off the grass. William put Grandfather down among the dark, damp branches behind the coal bunker.

"Time you went to bed,' he said, "or Hoppity will get you."

Hoppity was a one-legged thrush who liked snails as much as William, but in a different way. There were so many dangers for snails. William tried to guard against them all.

Grandfather made his way slowly down the layers of dead branches with his family following him, looking well-dressed and unusual. William picked up his bag of bottle tops and tube caps, scissors and sellotape and went indoors. Snails sleep by day.

That evening, his mother said, "There's a surprise tonight."

"What?" cried William.

"Look out of the window and see what Daddy's doing!"

"A bonfire!"

"Yes, and you can take the matches out now and tell Daddy to light it."

The bonfire was taller than William. All the summer prunings were on it and the poor brown Christmas tree. His father struck a match. His mother brought out a tray of baked potatoes wrapped in red serviettes. Crackles and pops began, wisps of smoke curled up. An orange glow began in the heart of the pile.

"Where did you get all the wood from?" asked William.

"From behind the coal bunker,' said his father. "I've been throwing dead branches there all summer."

"Oh no,' shouted William, jumping up.

"Careful,' shouted his father. "Don't pull branches out of the fire, you'll get burnt."

"My snails are there,' wailed William. "You've taken their home. There's Grandfather just waking up.

A red military hat was moving slowly through the smoke. Other hats began to emerge. Mother Snail in her pink Smartie top, Auntie in her modish white medicine bottle hat, three young snails in jaunty toothpaste caps, red green and blue.

"Snails in hats!" cried William's father. "Am I seeing things?"

The snails crawled upwards leaving their homes which had been so safe and dark and were now so hot and bright.

"Quick, William, get the long, metal tongs from the kitchen,' called his mother. William raced into the kitchen, got the tongs and tore back with them.

His father took them and carefully lifted Grandfather off his branch just as the flame ran up it. William tipped the potatoes off the tray and held it out. Grandfather shrank into his shell at the touch of the cool tray. Mother Snail was rescued, then Auntie, then the three young snails, clinging to a smouldering branch. William carried them over on the tray to the deep black shadow under the black currant bushes and put each one down in the dewy grass.

"You've had a nasty fright,' he told them soothingly,"but you'll be all right now.!

Then he went back to the bonfire. His father was already rebuilding it, his mother had taken the tray in to wash it. William searched for the fallen potatoes, and rubbed the ash off them.

"I don't know whether you ought to put hats on snails,' said his mother coming out with hot cocoa.

"It saved their lives,' said William. "We saw them in the smoke, and it makes Hoppity think twice."

"Well,' said his mother, "I don't know. They must feel heavy. But I'm glad we saved them, even though they do eat my lupins."

Then they stood round the fire eating hot potatoes and drinking cocoa, while behind them under the blackcurrant bushes Grandfather led his family into the cool delicious darkness to forage for food.

June Counsel

Counting Sheep

Wes Magee

They said,
"If you can't get to sleep
try counting sheep."
I tried.
It didn't work.

They said,
"Still awake? Count rabbits, dogs
Or leaping frogs."
I tried.
It didn't work.

They said,
"It's very late. Count rats,
or red-eyed bats!"
I tried.
It didn't work.

They said,
"Stop counting stupid sheep!
EYES CLOSED! DON'T PEEP!"
I tried
and fell asleep.

Wes Magee

Simon's Monster

Hazel Townson

"Don't go near the canal! said Simon's mum.

She said this ten times a day to Simon's big sisters, Trish and Paula. Trish and Paula had to look after Simon and keep him safe from harm.

Mum put on Simon's jacket and combed his hair. Then she said to the girls again:

"Remember now, keep away from that canal!"

Simon did not know what a canal was. How could he know if he never saw it? He guessed it was a huge and frightening monster in a lair near Curran's mill. Sometimes he heard it roaring. One dark, windy night it came galloping up the lane towards their house, hungry and angry. A good thing the door was locked and the curtains drawn.

Trish and Paula took Simon to the library.

"Simon can have a book with one of my tickets", said Trish.

"He can't read."

"Well, he can look at the pictures. What sort of book do you want, Simon?"

"A book about a canal."

"No," said Trish. "There's only one book about a canal. It's too boring. You won't like it."

Simon knew what boring meant. He had watched his dad boring holes. Perhaps the canal bored holes in people with its horns. Trish was right; he would not like that.

"Here's a good book for Simon," said Paula.

The cover of the book had a picture of a great, green dragon roaring across a river.

"Is that a canal?" asked Simon.

"Well, it's nearly the same," said Paula, thinking he meant the river.

"You and your canal!" sighed Trish.

Next day, Gran came from London for a holiday.

Gran loved the country.

"We shall go out every day," she said to Simon.

When Trish and Paula were at school, Gran and Simon had fun.

They went to the park. They rambled through the woods. They climbed up the hill behind Simon's house. Then, one lunchtime,

Gran said they would walk by the canal that afternoon.

Simon looked startled. His tummy felt queer and he could not eat his pudding.

"Aren't you scared, Gran?"

"Scared of a weedy old canal? I should just think not!" said Gran.

So the monster was not frightening after all. It was growing old, losing its strength. Simon began to feel sorry for it.

Gran and Simon walked through the fields. They came to Curran's mill. The mill stood on the banks of the water and the power from the water ran the mill. Simon did not feel scared with Gran beside him. Gran had her umbrella.

"Where's the canal?" asked Simon.

"Right in front of you, of course!" Gran pointed with her umbrella.

"Oh!" said Simon. He could see nothing but water. Then he knew! The monster was invisible. It could see them, but they could not see it. The monster hummed quietly to itself. But it did not try to hurt them; it was old.

At teatime, Simon said: "They'll never be able to catch it, anyway."

"Catch what, dear?"

"The canal."

Trish and Paula giggled. "Isn't he funny, mum? Who would ever want to catch a canal?"

"Good!" thought Simon. "Nobody wants to catch the canal. And the canal does not want to catch us."

"I'd like another piece of cake," said Simon. "Please!"

Hazel Townson

Thoughts Like An Ocean

Gareth Owen

The sea comes to me on the shore
On lacy slippered feet
And shyly, slyly slides away
With a murmur of defeat

And as I stand there wondering
Strange thoughts spin round my head
Of why and where and what and when
And if not, why, what then?

Where do lobsters come from?
And where anemones?
And are there other worlds out there
With other mysteries?

Why do I walk upon dry land
While fishes haunt the sea?
And as I think about their lives
Do they too think of me?

Why is water, water?
Why does it wet my hand?
Are there really as many stars
As there are grains of sand?

And where would the ocean go to
If there were no gravity?
And where was I before I lived?
And where's eternity?

Perhaps the beach I'm standing on
Perhaps this stretch of sand
Perhaps the Universe itself
Lies on someone else's hand?

And isn't it strange how this water and I
At this moment happened to meet
And how this tide sweeps half the world
Before stopping at my feet.

Animal Chatter

Gyles Brandreth

The other morning, feeling dog-tired, I was walking sluggishly to school,
When I happened upon two girls I know - who were busy playing the fool.
They were monkeying about, having a fight -
But all that they said didn't sound quite right.
"You're batty, you are - and you're catty too."
"That's better than being ratty, you peevish shrew!"
"Don't be so waspish!" "Don't be such a pig!"
"Look who's getting cocky - your head's too big!"
"You silly goose! Let me have my say!"
"Why should I, you elephantine popinjay?!"
I stopped, I looked, I listened - and I had to laugh
Because I realised then, of course, it's never the cow or the calf
That behave in this bovine way.
It's mulish humans like those girls I met the other day.
You may think I'm dogged, but something fishy's going on -
The way we beastly people speak of animals is definitely wrong.
Crabs are rarely crabby and mice are never mousey
(And I believe all lice deny that they are lousy).
you know, if I wasn't so sheepish and if I had my way
I'd report the English language to the RSPCA.

The Dog in the Basement

Angela Bull

The dog lay in a corner, between the kitchen door, and the bottom of the basement stairs. His red eyes rolled. His nose snuffled. He looked just ready to bite the little servant girl, as she scurried from the kitchen to the staircase.

The girl was called Mary. She was thirteen, and she had arrived that morning from her home in the country, as girls used to do a long time ago, to work as a maid in a big house in town. Mary had never seen anywhere so grand. There were seventy-six stairs to climb, from the basement kitchen where she was to help a fat Cook in a gravy-stained apron, to the attic bedroom which she had to share with another maid, Lizzie.

Mary didn't mind sharing, but she did mind Lizzie. Lizzie had a sharp face, and eyes like hard, bright chips of coal. Her skinny body tapered down to matchstick ankles, and enormous feet. Lizzie warned Mary about the dog, while Mary put on her black maid's dress and white apron.

"He'll tear your leg open if you let him, Rex will. You've got to skip past like lightning. The girl before you - he bit off two of her toes. I heard him crunching them."

Dogs frightened Mary. She knew it was silly, but she couldn't help it. So a fierce dog, as well as a new job in a strange house, seemed the last straw.

Added to which, there was to be a dinner party that night. As soon as Mary had returned to the kitchen in her maid's clothes, she was given a pile of muddy potatoes to peel.

"Do them nicely, or Cook'll box your ears," hissed Lizzie. "She's got a terrible temper, so watch out!"

Luckily the kitchen sink was in a dark corner. Nobody could see the tears which ran down Mary's nose into the muddy potato water. A cross Cook, and a fierce dog! If only she was back at home!

Then it was time to lay the dinner table for the party. "Be quick about it, or there'll be trouble," threatened Lizzie.

Mary scuttled up and down the basement stairs with trays of plates and cutlery. Every time she passed Rex, his bristling nose inched forward, and his red eyes stared. "You've forgotten the rolls!" called Lizzie from the kitchen.

She thrust a basketful into Mary's hands. Rex's whole nose was on the bottom step. He snuffled noisily. Mary jumped, and rolls flew everywhere. She scrambled them together, blew the dust off, and raced upstairs.

A butler was in charge of the dining room. "Put the basket here," he said, quite pleasantly.

Mary placed it on the table, and hurried back to the basement stairs. Rex's head lolled across the step. Mary screwed up her courage, jumped over him, and dashed, trembling, into the kitchen. "He nearly got your toes then!" whispered Lizzie, who was on her way up to the dining room. "Well," said Cook. She was decorating a trifle, but she looked up, and for the first time Mary saw her friendly face. "You've made a good start. I've never known the table laid so quickly. Here." She held out a candied cherry. Mary popped it in her mouth. It was delicious. Cook was beaming. Mary suddenly knew she'd never box anyone's ears. "Take that last dish up, love' said Cook.

Rex's red eyes rolled up at Mary from the bottom step. But - I've passed him lots of times, and he hasn't even bared his teeth, Mary realised. Had Lizzie invented his fierceness, like she'd invented Cook's crossness, because she was a bully, and enjoyed alarming people? Mary laid a timid hand on Rex's head. His red eyes rolled lovingly towards her. He dribbled happily.

Mary saw Lizzie's matchstick ankles and enormous feet, coming towards her down the stairs. "Liar!" said Mary; and she skipped, smiling, up to the dining room with her dish.

Angela Bull

Where is my Wig ?

Pam Ayres

I had a horse called Blackie
Though he was mainly white
He and me we galloped free
On many a rainy night.

One night we galloped madly
My wig flew in the air
I looked for it all morning
Have you seen it anywhere?

The Leader

Roger McGough

I wanna be the leader
I wanna be the leader
Can I be the leader?
Can I? I can?
Promise? Promise?
Yippee, I'm the leader
I'm the leader
OK what shall we do?

Silly Poem

Brian Cant

On a Saturday night in the Desert,
As the sun sank low in the West
A ginger-haired man, smoking Kippers,
Strolled round in his pants and his vest.

His name was Alfonso McGregor
A Spaniard born in Dunoon
And because he did everything slowly
He always ate soup with a fork.

He found his way into the desert
When he strayed from a British Rail tour
Which started from Penge one morning in Spring
And returned at a quarter to four.

He was lost, he was frightened
It slowly grew dark.
No more light than a very small candle
When a camel strolled up -
Gave his ankle a lick
And swallowed the heel off his sandal.

THANK YOU,

Brian Cant

(exit quickly because listeners to this poem
are prone to throw things!)

Poem

Victoria Wood

There was a boy who didn't like poems

didn't like poems

didn't like veg

didn't like music

didn't like jokes

didn't like fun

didn't like knees

didn't like Cubs

but when he was 28,

well, nearly 29 -

he cheered UP!

Victoria Wood

The Evening Is Coming *Anon*

The evening is coming,
The sun sinks to rest,
The birds are a flying
Straight home to their nests.
"Caw, Caw", says the Crow,
As he flies overhead,
"It's time little children
Were going to bed".

Here comes the pony.
His work is all done.
Down through the meadow,
He takes a good run.
Up goes his heels,
And down goes his head.
It's time little children
Were going to bed.

Anon

The Dusty Gran

Pam Ayres

Dust was lying very thick
On my granny's shooting stick,
Thicker still upon the stair
And on my granny's silver hair.
From her dust-encrusted knees
Fell a plate of bread and cheese
"How are you dear Gran?"I cried,
"Ah, not so dusty". She replied.

Fat Cat

Mary Rayner

Siamese have cobalt eyes, their tails are thin and kinky,
Siamese are slender, Siamese are slinky,
The experts are agreed on that –
They haven't seen this family cat.

His fur is sleek, his eyes are blue,
His pedigree is long and true,
But what a figure! What a weight!
And how he eats! At what rate!
For pussy hasn't read the books,
He doesn't know how wrong he looks.

Left-over yogurt, frozen peas,
Spaghetti, any kind if cheese,
He wolfs them down (if that's the word)
Then ups and outs and grabs a bird.
He sits below the baby's chair
To catch the dropped bits in the air,
The phone rings and you turn your back,
He's on the table, snicker snack.

We tried to keep him slim and lean,
He got bad -tempered, scratchy, mean,
And used to tour the neighbours' bins
And leave bits – fish bones and skins-
On our front doorstep. And one time
He stole their Sunday joint, a crime
We really felt must be prevented;
So now he's fat, full and contented,
The Siamese who over-ate,
Our greedy,gross,unusual pet.

Peregrine and the Amazingly Useful Present

Linda Mori

Peregrine slowly opened one eye, then quickly closed it again. 'Just five minutes more', he thought, snuggling down underneath the quilt. He felt like a little hedgehog, curled up inside a cosy hold at the bottom of a tree. Just as he was wondering whether he would have enough nuts to eat that day, he heard his mum's voice calling up the stairs.

'Peregrine! Wake up at once, we're late for school!' Peregrine crawled out of bed and shivered. He began to get dressed but, as usual, he could only find one sock. 'Oh, no, not again!' he thought. He wished his mum would be a bit tidier about the house and know where important things were, like socks. His best friend, Alastair, had a very tidy mum. She always knew where everything was, even scissors and sellotape, which Peregrine's mum could never find. Sighing, he went to the airing cupboard and opened the door. An enormous pile of vests, odd socks, shirts, dresses and towels fell on top of him. He crawled through the jungle of clothes and finally found the missing sock.

'Peregrine! Aren't you washed yet?' shouted Mum. Peregrine dashed into the bathroom and two minutes later was downstairs munching his 'Chocopops' for breakfast.

'I hope you remembered to clean your teeth properly today, Peregrine', said Dad from behind the newspaper. 'You're eight years old now and I shouldn't have to remind you.' Before Peregrine could reply, he heard the plop of a letter landing on the doormat.

'I'll get it!' he cried, running into the hall. He always hoped there would be a letter for him, but there never was. Mum said that if he wanted a letter, he'd have to write to somebody first, but Peregrine couldn't think of anybody to write to. He picked up the letter and looked at it. It looked extremely interesting. It had seven stamps, all in a row, and the word 'AMERICA' printed at the top. It was addressed to "MR. HENRY PARKER, 24, WALNUT ROAD,

SILVERTHORPE, ENGLAND," so Peregrine gave it to Dad.

'Hmm, America eh? I wonder who it's from', said Dad. He started to read the letter and began chuckling and talking to himself.' Well fancy that! Well I never! Goodness gracious me!'

'For heaven's sake, tell us who it's from!' cried Mum.

'It's from my cousin, Professor Wilbur J. Jackson, the famous computer scientist. He says he's going to send a present to our Peregrine! Here, Peregrine, read this bit', said Dad, handing him the letter.

The letter said: *'I am sending you an amazingly useful present. I use mine nearly every day. It is the best in the world and will last for years and years. Please write soon to say how you like it. Yours affectionately, Cousin Wilbur XXXXXX'*

Peregrine was thrilled to bits and his heart started beating faster and faster. He knew at once what the present would be – a computer, of course! It just had to be the Zircon XZ eleven. Why, only yesterday he had seen an advert for it on television which said that the Zircon was the best and most amazingly useful computer in the world and would last for years and years. Peregrine knew that some computers played chess with you. He wondered whether the Zircon could play snakes and ladders with him. He also wondered whether he could use it to help Mum remember where she put things in the house. Yesterday he had asked Mum and Dad whether he could have a computer for his next birthday but they had said he would have to wait for a few years. But now he was going to get one after all – good old Cousin Wilbur!

One week later a huge wooden crate arrived from America, addressed to Peregrine. It had lots of stickers all over it which said 'FRAGILE – WITH CARE'. 'I hope my computer isn't broken', thought Peregrine worriedly. Mum and Dad helped Peregrine get the lid off with screwdrivers. Inside was lots of plastic paper with little bubbles in it. Underneath that was a cardboard box. Dad carefully lifted it out onto the carpet. It was exactly the right size and shape for a computer. Peregrine's heart was thumping again as he lifted the lid and found inside. . . . . . twelve big red books with gold writing on the front, lying side by side. Peregrine could hardly believe his eyes. Slowly, he picked up one of the books and read the title. It said, *"Wonderworld Encylclopaedia. Everything anybody wants to know in the whole wide world."* Peregrine didn't speak, but his Mum did.

'Oh, Peregrine, arn't they beautiful – just smell the leather! You're going to find them so useful. Help me put them in the bookcase!'

When they had finished, Peregrine had to agree that the encyclopaedias did look very smart and they smelled lovely, too, but he just couldn't think what he would use them for. 'Oh, well, never mind', he sighed, 'it was kind of Cousin Wilbur and maybe I'll get a computer one day.'

After tea, Peregrine was watching one of his favourite programmes, 'Junior Mastermind! Children had to answer questions about their favourite subject. The question-master was called Fergus Ferguson and he always wore a big bow-tie.

At the end of every programme there was a competition for children watching at home. Fergus would ask a question and the first child to send him the correct answer would win a prize. It was a different prize every week. Peregrine had always wanted to win one of the prizes, but he could never answer the question, and neither could Mum or Dad.

Today, Fergus said, 'This week's fabulous prize is the most amazingly useful computer, the Zircon XZ eleven!' Peregrine could hardly believe his ears! He jumped up and ran over to the television. He was going to win that prize!

'Now listen carefully to this week's question', Fergus was saying. 'Two men invented the world's first automatic, electronic, digital computer. What were their names? The first person to send me the correct answer will win the Zircon computer!'

Peregrine screwed up his eyes and thought and thought and thought, but it was no use. He knew he didn't know the answer. How could he find out? Suddenly, out of the corner of his eye, he noticed something red and gold. Of course! The Wonderworld Encyclopaedias! He thought as fast as he could. 'Now, 'computer' begins with 'c'.' He found the book marked with a 'c' at the bottom, and quickly

turned the pages until he found the word 'computer'. He began reading. It said, 'the first automatic, electronic, digital computer was invented by John W. Mauchly and J. Prosper Eckert.'

'Mum, Mum! I've got the answer!' yelled Peregrine, running into the kitchen. When he'd told her all about it, she was just as excited as Peregrine! Mum managed to find a postcard and a stamp and Peregrine carefully copied the names of the men in his very best writing. Then Mum helped him address the card to Fergus Ferguson at the television studios in London.

'Quick, we'd better hurry and post it before the last collection at six o'clock', Mum said. They ran faster than they'd ever run before and got to the letter box just as the postman was emptying the letters into his sack!

All the next week, Peregrine kept wondering whether he had won the computer. He knew he had the right answer, but was his postcard the first to reach Fergus? At last it was time for 'Junior Mastermind'. Peregrine, Mum and Dad sat on the edge of the settee as Fergus Ferguson said, 'Now I will tell you who has won the Zircon XZ eleven. The winner is ... now let me see ... ah, yes, Peregrine Parker of 24, Walnut Road, Silverthorpe. Congratulations, Peregrine!'

Peregrine, Mum and Dad jumped up and down and hugged each other. 'I must write to Cousin Wilbur right now', cried Peregrine, dashing to get his pen and paper. He began to write, *'Dear Cousin Wilbur, Thank you very much for the encyclopaedias. I have found them amazingly useful already . . .'*

Linda Mort

What do you get if you cross an  with a computer?

A 4-ton know-all!

My Robot *Michael Rosen*

Once I made a robot
out of boxes and of cans
with buttons for its eyes
wooden spoons for its hands.

It's mouth was a Macdonald's box
that opened and then shut.
One day I wasn't looking
and it bonked me on the nut!

Michael Rosen

The Baked Bean Tree

Anne Rooke

'What are baked beans really?' Tom asked looking at his supper one Monday evening.

'Well, they're beans in tomato sauce,' said his father.

'Yes. But what are beans?' asked Tom again.

'Beans are seeds,' said his father. 'Put them in the ground and they grow,' he said.

'GOOD,' said Tom.

On Tuesday Tom opened the kitchen cupboard and took out a tin of baked beans.

He walked down to the end of the garden – right down to the far end where the nettles and dock leaves grew and nobody ever went. And there, in the damp earth, he planted that tin of baked beans. Dig – dig. Pat – pat. Stamp – stamp.

'GOOD,' said Tom.

On Wednesday Tom walked down the garden with his eyes shut ready for a surprise.

He got it.

The baked bean tree was as tall as him. It was covered in glossy green leaves and several tins of baked beans.

Tom picked the tins of beans and carried them up to the kitchen.

He stacked them neatly in the kitchen cupboard.

'Heavens!' said his mother when she opened the cupboard that evening. 'Fancy that.'

'GOOD,' said Tom.

HEINZ
BAKED
BEANS

On Thursday Tom ran down the garden with a basket.

The baked bean tree was twice as tall as he was. And it had more glossy green leaves and many more tins of baked beans.

Tom picked the tins of baked beans and put them in his basket.

Then he carried them to his grandmother's house.

'Sakes alive!' said his grandmother when she saw the beans.

'You'll have to come and help me eat them, Tom,' she said.

'GOOD,' said Tom.

On Friday Tom trundled down the garden with a wheelbarrow. The baked bean tree was three times as tall as he was. it was covered in glossy green leaves and huge numbers of baked beans. Tom picked the tins of beans and put them in his wheelbarrow. The he trundled the wheelbarrow along to the school.

'I do declare!' said Mrs O'Halloran the dinner lady when she saw the beans. 'The teachers will have to help me open them.'

'GOOD,' said Tom.

On Saturday Tom went to play at his grandmother's house and he did not go down the garden until the afternoon.

The baked bean tree was four times as tall as he was and covered in dark green leaves and hundreds of tins of baked beans.

Four times Tom filled his wheelbarrow with tins of baked beans.

And four times he wheeled his barrow down the hill to the church.

'God bless my soul!' said the vicar. 'What a gift for the harvest festival.'

'GOOD,' said Tom.

On Sunday Tom went to church for the harvest festival.

'What happens if a farmer does not pick his apples?' Tom asked the vicar.

'The apples would fall of the trees when the winter comes,' said the vicar. 'But , of course, new apples would grow next year,' he added.

'And what happens,' Tom went on, 'If a farmer does not pick his beans?'

'Ah,' said the vicar, 'Then the beans would wither and harden and the plants would shrivel away. That would be sad. But the squirrels could gather the hard beans for their winter food. And that would gladden their hearts.'

'GOOD,' said Tom.

On Monday Tom said to his father, 'Is winter coming soon?'

'Yes,' said his father.

'Do squirrels like baked beans?' asked Tom.

'Yes,' said his father.

'May I have spaghetti for supper?' asked Tom.

'Yes,' said his father.

'What is spaghetti really?' asked Tom.

'It's flour and eggs,' said his father.

'Does it grow on trees?' asked Tom.

'No,' said his father.

'GOOD,' said Tom.

Anne Rooke

Fairy Story

Tony Ross

Annie stood still as a stone. She was sure that something moved, in the darkest corner of the shed, amongst the plastic flower pots. There it was again.

Annie crept forward, quietly, holding out her hands, she was SURE it was a dragonfly, trapped in the old shed. SLO..W..L..Y...

... then Annie pushed aside the flower pots, and stared.

Staring back, and shivering with fright, was a tiny girl. She was dressed in a thin yellow dress, and a pair of shiny wings drooped down her back.

Annie didn't quite believe in fairies, but she had to ask;

"Er, you're not a FAIRY are you?"

"What d'ye think I am, a bicycle pump?" snapped the small creature rudely.

"OF COURSE I'm a fairy."

The fairy had stopped shaking now, and was glaring up at Annie. With a whoop, Annie grabbed her new find and held her in cupped hands.

"HOI!" screeched the fairy.

"Put me DOWN, you great clumsy..."

Then the fairy shouted out such rude names that Annie was quite shocked. She never guessed that fairies knew such words.

"A FAIRY!" shouted Annie. "I've caught a FAIRY. I'LL BE RICH AND FAMOUS!"

"GET LOST!" yelled the fairy, and bit Annie's finger.

Annie popped the fairy into an empty jam jar, and slipped on the lid. Then she poked some airholes in the lid with a nail. The fairy wiggled her nose, and put out her tongue.

Annie rushed indoors, waving the jam jar.

"MUM ... I've got a FAIRY!"

Annie's mum smiled.

"So you have dear," she said, without looking at the jar.

"Don't forget to wash your hands after being in the garden."

Mum went on writing her letter to Auntie Edie.

Annie rushed into the dining room, where dad was painting the skirting board.

"Dad," she shouted. "Do you want to see a FAIRY?"

"Not right now", said dad.

"DON'T STEP ON THAT PAPER!"

Annie ran back into the garden, just as a policeman was passing,

'"Look," said Annie, "I've caught a FAIRY!"

"Yes luv," grinned the policeman, and strolled on his way.

Annie swung on the garden gate, clutching the jar. The fairy was hopping mad now, and shouting rude words again.

Annie's teacher was the next to pass the garden.

"Want to listen to a FAIRY?" said Annie.

"I'm sure it's very interesting dear," said her teacher, walking by, without a glance at the jam jar.

Annie sighed, and walked slowly back into the shed. She put the jar on the floor, by the flower pots, and took off the lid.

"Can I go in?" said the fairy.

"You may as well," said Anne. "I'd have thought people would have been more interested in you."

The fairy fluttered up into the air, stardust swirling from her wings.

"Grown-ups are always like that," she laughed. "Sorry I bit your finger."

Then ... Annie's fairy was gone.

My Outfits

Chris Powling

My clown outfit makes Dad smile.
My monster outfit makes Mum yell.
My pirate outfit makes Grandpa say "Yo-ho-ho!"
My Royal outfit makes Grandma curtsey.
My teacher outfit makes my little sister giggle.
My disco outfit makes my big brother dance.
My lion-tamer outfit makes my dog bark and bark and bark.
But under all the outfits
It's only me.

Chris Powling

Mr Podmore *Robin Kingsland*

For as long as most people could remember, Mr. and Mrs. Percy Podmore had looked after the little shop at the end of the road.

Each day Mrs. Podmore, in her blue overall, would stand behind the shop counter, selling newspapers, sweets and colouring books, while Mr. Percy Podmore sat on a stool in a closed-off part of the shop, where he would sell stamps, make up postal orders, and weight parcels.

When he came to work, Mr. Percy Podmore always wore; a grey shirt with a blue tie, black trousers, and little round silver spectacles … until …

One day Mr. Podmore decided that he was going to start wearing some different clothes;

New clothes...

Colourful clothes....

DAZZLING CLOTHES!!!

Next day, when Mr. Podmore opened up his little office, he was not wearing his blue tie. Instead, Mr. Podmore had on an eye-catching, rainbow coloured bow tie.

"It's very bright, dear," said Mrs. Podmore. "It will cheer up the customers when they see it," said Mr. Podmore, smiling.

But Mr. Podmore's tie didn't just cheer people up. It actually made them laugh!

They laughed so much that they forgot what they had come in for.

They laughed so much that they took ages to buy their stamps, and people queueing behind them grumbled.

They laughed so much that people at the back of the queue tried to push forward to see what was so funny, and the people in front of them got annoyed.

At lunchtime, Mrs. Podmore begged her husband to change into his old blue tie again. He was very disappointed, but he had to admit that his bow-tie had caused far too much commotion.

Still Mr. Podmore wanted to wear brighter clothes. So the following Sunday, when the shop was closed, Mr. Podmore put on a stripy Tee-shirt, a pair of yellow shorts, and his luminous green spectacles, and took the dog for a walk.

Poor Mr. Podmore! Everywhere he went he could hear people whispering to each other as he went past.

"How ridiculous," they said.

"At his age too,"

"If my Albert went out like that I don't know WHAT I'd do!"

"It's his good lady I feel sorry for!"

When he got home, Mr. Podmore changed into his old clothes. He spent the rest of the day in the back garden digging weeds, and frowning.

Mr. Podmore was terribly disappointed. All he wanted to do was to wear something colourful for a change, but every time he tried, people complained. What could he do?

On Wednesday the vicar came into the shop. He was organising the village fete. The main event was to be a fancy dress

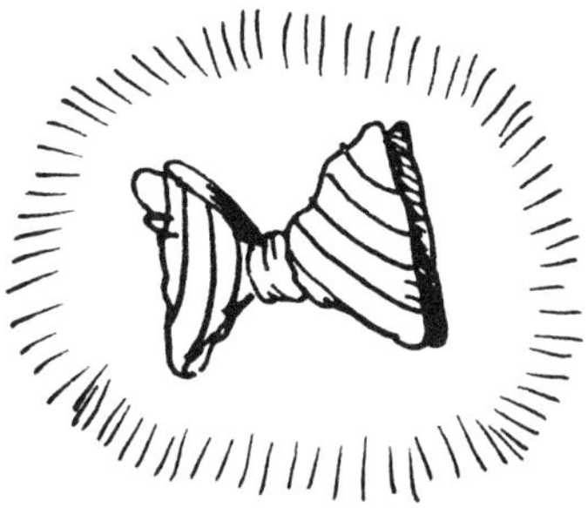

parade for the children. They were going to be led through the High Street in their costumes by Mr. Top-Hat, a famous clown. The posters had been up for weeks.

"But now Mr. Top-Hat is ill," said the vicar, "so he won't be able to come. The children will be so disappointed. They do love Mr. Top-Hat and his colour ful costumes."

Mr. Podmore was out of his little office in a moment.

"I'd be happy to lead the parade," he said, "That is, if you'd like me to." "I'd be delighted," said the vicar, "but are you sure you don't mind wearing a clown's costume?" "MIND?" cried Mr. Podmore, "Not at all. Not at ALL!"

On the day of the parade Mr. Podmore was DAZZLING, and he made everyone laugh and clap as he led the children happily down the high street in his costume.

"Hooray for Mr. Podmore," sang the children.

"Hooray for Mr. Podmore," everybody cheered.

"Hooray for Mr. Podmore," called Mrs. Podmore, waving from the crowd.

Nowadays, whatever he's doing, Mr. Podmore always wears a bright bow tie, or a patterned shirt, or a multi-coloured scarf. And no-one whispers when he walks the dog, unless it's to say: "I must ask Mr. Podmore where he bought that wonderful pullover."

In fact these days the whole town is trying to be as colourful as Mr. Podmore.

But, every summer, when the day of the fete comes around, who is it who dresses up in his bright clown clothes and makes everyone cheer and laugh as he leads the parade?

Who do you think?

Robin Kingsland

Rodge Said *Michael Rosen*

Rodge said,
  'Teachers — they want it all ways'.
You're jumping up and down on a chair
or something
and they grab hold of you and say
  "Would you do that sort of thing in your own home?"

'So you say, "No"
And they say,
  "Well don't do it here then."

'But if you say, "Yes, I do it at home."
they say
  "Well, we don't want that sort of thing
going on here
thank you very much"

'Teachers — they get you all ways'.
Rodge said

Michael Rosen

Footsteps

Barbara Ireson

Our lawn, which yesterday was green,
Today is nowhere to be seen.
The snow fell heavily all night
Leaving a covering of white.
It's smooth as icing and as clean.
Nothing has spoiled it. No one's seen.
But in a minute I shall go
In Wellingtons across the snow
And every footstep that I take
Will spoil the icing on the cake.

Barbara Ireson

The Little Fish *Tony Bradman*

I am a little fishy
I live down in the sea
I swim around
Without a sound
I like being me.

Tony Bradman

Sunshine and Showers *Pam Ramage*

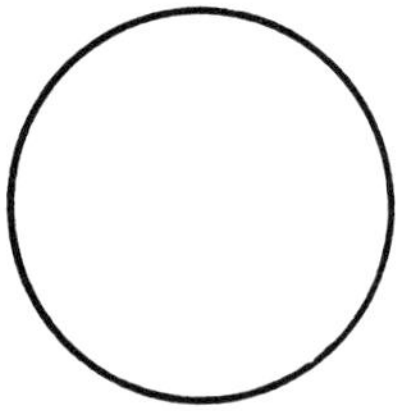

It was lovely sunny weather. Jenny and Tom played outside every day. "I wish the sun could shine all the time," said Jenny. "Nobody would miss the horrible old rain," said Tom.

Day after day, the sun shone brightly. Everybody was enjoying the hot weather and nobody seemed to miss the rain. Jenny put out a bowl of water for the birds, because all the streams were drying up. Tom helped his dad water the garden as the plants and flowers were beginning to droop. The weeks went by and still no rain fell. "I'm fed up going for picnics," grumbled Jenny. "It's too hot to play outside," complained Tom. "The garden is too dry for digging," said dad. It was even too hot for gran to go for a walk or sit outside. Jenny wanted to fill an old basin with water and paddle in it. "I'll' water the flowers with the garden hose," said Tom. "You can't have any water, dad told them. "We have to save it because the water supply is very low. We need the rain to fill up the reservoir again."

"We need the rain as much as the sun, then' said Tom. "That's

right," said gran. "The farmers need rain or their crops won't grow." "I wish it would rain," said Jenny. Next day a big black cloud hid the sun. "It's going to rain!" shouted Tom and it did. When the rain stopped, everything was damp and fresh again. Jenny and Tom splashed in all the puddles. Their gran went for a long walk and the garden was just right for digging.

Pam Ramage

Holiday by the Sea *Sheila Lavelle*

Ben and Lucy were sulking. Everybody was going on holiday except them. Mum had no money for holidays this year.

"It's not fair," wailed Lucy. "Why can't we go camping at the seaside?"

"Sorry, kids," said Mum. "It would cost about a hundred pounds. We'll go next year, I promise."

Mum went outside to make a new garden path. Ben and Lucy played on the swing and tried not to think about the seaside.

At ten o'clock a lorry stopped outside the house. "This must be the sand for my path," said Mum.

The lorry tipped a mountain of yellow sand into the front garden. Then it drove away.

"It's just like the seaside," said Ben.

"So it is!" laughed Mum. She spread out the pile of sand and raked it smooth.

"That's the beach," she said.

Then Mum brought out the paddling pool and filled it with water from the garden hose.

"That's the sea," she said.

Ben and Lucy put on their bathing suits and paddled in the pool.

Mum wore her sunglasses and her straw hat. She sat in a deck-chair and did her knitting.

The children played in the sand with buckets and spades. They made an enormous sandcastle. Mum made a flag for the top with a lollipop stick and a paper hanky.

All the neighbours came to stare over the wall.

"The Jones's are on holiday," said Mrs Brown.

"They didn't tell me they were going," said the milkman.

At lunchtime they had fish and chips from the shop round the corner. They sat on a rug and ate them straight out of the paper, and they were delicious.

"I always feel hungry at the seaside," said Mum. And when the ice-cream man came she went out and bought three ice-creams.

"This is just as good as the real seaside," said Lucy, licking her ice-cream.

Ben thought of the real seaside. He thought of the waves and the seagulls and the wonderful smell of seaweed. "It's not really as good," he said. "But it's better than nothing, I suppose."

In the afternoon a van came along the road. "BBC Television it said on the front. It stopped outside the Jones's garden and two men got out. One of them had a TV camera.

"Will you let us make a film of you for the Holiday Show?" they said to Mum. "We'll pay you a small fee."

Nobody minded at all. And when the filming was over the TV men game Mum a bit of paper. Then they drove away.

Mum looked at the paper.

"Ben! Lucy! Look at this!" she said. "It's a cheque for a hundred pounds." She hugged Ben and Lucy in delight. "Now we can go to the real seaside after all."

"Hooray"' shouted Ben and Lucy, dancing round the garden. "When can we go?"

"Just as soon as we've packed our bags," said Mum. "Come on, I'll race you upstairs!"

Sheila Lavelle

Fish Face *Floella Benjamin*

It's lots of fun to be a fish
to swim so fast with a swishy swish

In an aquarium we sometimes stay
and people see us every day

They watch us as we swim and swim,
round plants and rocks and shells within.

Our shiny scales their colours glow
like a multi-coloured rainbow show

Our funny faces make you smile
as you stand and watch us for a while

But you're just as funny don't you know
so we look at you and say "Ho' "Ho'.

Floella Benjamin

School Day?

Jennifer A. Lockwood

Jump out of bed -
A bright new day.
Into the bathroom,
Without delay.

Back to my bedroom,
Pull on two socks.
Take off my nightie,
Quick as a fox.

Into my pants,
Arms into my vest.
Even a petticoat,
To cover my chest.

Into my school skirt,
And school jumper too,
Feeling so glad
I've no buttons to do.

A brush for my hair,
Comb it all through.
I'll leave my ribbons
For Mummy to do.

Into my black shoes,
Fasten each lace.
Speedily dressed
With a smile on my face.

Out of the bedroom,
Stairs - two at a time.
Into the kitchen
As the clocks chime.

"Good morning' to Mummy,
"Good morning my dear,
You're ready for school ...
But it's SUNDAY, I fear!"

Jennifer A. Lockwood

The Lullaby Leopard

Adele Geras

Leopard was snoring so loudly that no-one in the jungle could sleep.

"My head seems to be quite near the stars," said Giraffe and he began to count them.

He had counted ten stars when a roaring snore disturbed him so much, he had to start again.

"We can't sleep, Momma. We want a drink!" said all the little elephants.

So Mamma Elephant put the kettle on for a cup of tea.

The tea was nearly ready when a snuffly snore made Momma Elephant jump, she dropped a teacup.

It landed on Snake, who was curled up nearby. "Who does she think I am? A snail?" he muttered to himself.

"I can't sleep," said Tiger to his wife. "Maybe this would be a good time to learn the alphabet."

He paced up and down on padded paws, snarling "A..B..C..D' and then Leopard let out a grunting snore, and Tiger forgot which letter came next.

The jungle birds could not sleep and neither could the butterflies, and so, after a particularly grunting, snuffling, roaring snoring night, they flew far away. Only one humming-bird was left behind because she was too lazy to move.

"Something must be done," said Momma Elephant to her friends the next morning. "My children are bad-tempered and so am I. We all need sleep."

The animals sat down in a circle and thought and thought.

Suddenly, from the branches of a small tree came the voice of the humming-bird. "I have a plan. Leave it to mmmmmmee."

Then she buried her beak in the nearest flower.

That night, Giraffe, Momma Elephant and her six children, Tiger and his

wife and even Snake waited for the first snore. They hid behind some bushes near Leopard's tree, and their eyes shone in the dark as they looked through the leaves.

As soon as Leopard was asleep, the humming-bird flew down and began humming in his ear.

Leopard dreamed of his father, humming on his way to the water-hole.

He dreamed of his mother, who hummed as she hunted for food.

He dreamed of rainbow-coloured birds humming in a shady tree on a very hot afternoon.

He dreamed of a humming car he had once seen, where the jungle ended and the village began.

And then he started to snore, but he snored such a melodious, humming lullaby that the listening animals nearly fell asleep before they had reached their beds.

Everyone in the jungle slept sweetly, lulled by the lullaby Leopard.

The next day, Momma Elephant made a cake..

and invited all the animals to a party in honour of the humming-bird, who had promised to hum in Leopard's ear every night.

The birds and the butterflies returned to the jungle, and everyone slept happily ever after.

Adele Geras

A Wakeful Night *Hazel Townson*

One night, Best Doll could not sleep. She tossed and turned in the Toy Box. She woke all the other toys.

"This will never do!" cried the Musical-Box. "I'll play you a lullaby. That will make you sleep."

So the Talking-Book told a long, long story. Best Doll enjoyed the story — but she did not fall asleep.

"I'll keep on jumping over the side of the Toy Box," said the Woolly Sheep.

"Then you can count me every time I jump. That will make you sleep."

So the Woolly Sheep jumped and jumped until his legs were tired..

Best Doll enjoyed counting the jumps — but she did not fall asleep.

" I'll rock you to sleep," said the Rocking-Horse. "Climb onto my back!"

So Best Doll climbed onto Rocking-Horse's back and they rocked away in the moonlight.

Best Doll enjoyed the ride — but she did not fall asleep.

"I'll put a spell on you to make you sleep," said the Magic Box. He tossed up his wand and tapped Best Doll on the shoulder with it.

"Abracadabra — eyes shut tight —

Sleep and sleep all through the night!" chanted the Magic Box.

Best Doll enjoyed having a spell put on her — but she did not fall asleep.

"I'll yawn," said the Green Felt Crocodile.

"I'll yawn and yawn with my big jaws. That will surely make you sleep."

So the Green Felt Crocodile stood in front of Best Doll and he yawned and yawned until his jaws nearly came apart.

Best Doll enjoyed watching the yawns — but she did not fall asleep.

"Ah, well!" thought the Cuckoo-Clock at last, it's my turn now! I will make Best Doll fall asleep."

So Cuckoo-Clock called seven cuckoos, although it was only the middle of the night.

"Time to get up!" cried Trumpet, blowing his morning call.

"Time to get up!" cried all the other toys.

"Time to start another day!"

Whereupon Best Doll closed her eyes — and fell fast asleep

Hazel Townson

Jo *Barbara Ireson*

You say that Jo has made you late,
You say that Jo has dropped a plate.
You say he never leaves your side,
But when I'm here he seems to hide.
Sometimes I think he must be shy,
Or is it that he's very sly?
He breaks your toys, he picks my flowers,
He keeps you out for hours and hours.
Poor secret Jo, it seems a shame
He always has to take the blame.
I wonder is it really true
It's always him and never you?

Barbara Ireson

Bedtime

Eleanor Farjeon

Five minutes, five minutes more, please!
  Let me stay five minutes more!
Can't I just finish the castle
  I'm building on the floor?
Can't I just finish the story
  I'm reading here in my book?
Can't I just finish this bead-chain –
  It *almost* is finished, look!
Can't I just finish this game, please?
  When a game's once begun
It's a pity never to find out
  Whether you've lost or won.
Can't I just stay five minutes?
  Well, can't I stay just four?
Three minutes, then? Two minutes?
  Can't I stay one minute more?

Eleanor Farjeon

Acknowledgements

My grateful thanks go the the following writers and publishers who have kindly given their permission to reproduce copyright material, and to all the writers who have written stories and poems especially for this collection.

The Magic Recorder written and illustrated by Thelma Lambert © 1988.
The Whatsit by Tony Bradman from All Together, Now! by kind permission of the author and Viking Kestrel.
Sally won't you walk with me? and *Thoughts Like an Ocean* by Gareth Owen from Song of the City by kind permission of the author and Fontana.
The Balaclava Story by George Layton © 1975 by kind permission of the author and Longman Group UK Ltd.
Lies by Kit Wright from Rabbiting On by kind permission of William Collins Sons & Co Ltd.
Sick by Shel Silverstein from Where the Sidewalk Ends by kind permission of Jonathan Cape Ltd.
A Million Beer Can Rings by Catherine Storr.
It's My Kick Next by Michael Hardcastle © 1988.
Hello, I'm Home! by June Crebbin from the Jungle Sale by kind permission of Viking Kestrel © 1988.
Skipper and Sam the Lovely Surprise for Mum written and illustrated by Carolyn Dinan.
The Rescue by June Counsel.
Counting Sheep by Wes Magee from the Witch's Brew Cambridge University Press 1989.
Simon's Monster by Hazel Townson.
Animal Chatter by Gyles Brandreth.
A Dog in the Basement by Angela Bull.
Where is my Wig? by Pam Ayres ©1987.

The Leader by Roger McGough from Sky in the Pie by kind permission of the author and Puffin Books.
Silly Poem by Brian Cant.
Poem by Victoria Wood.
The Evening is Coming by Anon.
The Dusty Gran by Pam Ayres.
Fat Cat by Mary Rayner.
Peregrine and the Amazingly Useful Present by Linda Mort.
My Robort by Michael Rosen.
The Baked Bean Tree by Anne Rooke.
Fairy Story written and illustrated by Tony Ross with permission from Granada Television Ltd.
My Outfits by Chris Powling.
Mr Podmore written and illustrated by Robin Kingsland.
Footsteps by Barbara Ireson from Rhyme Time 2 published by Beaver Books.
Sunshine and Showers by Pam Ramage and illustrated by Charlotte Firmin reprinted by permission of Polystyle Publications Ltd.
Holiday by the Sea by Sheila Lavelle.
The Little Fish by Tony Bradman from Animals Like Us by kind permission of the author and Blackie & Son Ltd.
Fish Face! by Floella Benjamin.
School-Day? by Jennifer A. Lockwood.
The Lullaby Leopard by Adele Geras.
Bedtime by Eleanor Farjeon from the Children's Bells published by Oxford University Press.

Many thanks also to Martin Ursell, Amanda Harvey, Eva Palmer, Margaret Campbell, Lesley Harker, Joanne Hardwick and especially Carolyn Dinan and Sandra Shapiro for their illustrations.

There is also a record available for a £2.00 donation to the fund.

Send your £2.00 cheques or postal order made to:-

"David Rose Tay Sachs Fund"

and post to:-

130 Church Street, Eccles,

Manchester, M30 OLS.

NORTHERN CLASSIC REPRINTS

Northern Classic Reprints

The Manchester Man

(Mrs. G. Linnaeus Banks)

Re-printed from an 1896 illustrated edition — undoubtedly the finest limp-bound edition ever. Fascinating reading, includes Peterloo. Over 400 pages, wonderfully illustrated.

ISBN 1 872226 16 7 £4.95

The Manchester Rebels

(W Harrison Ainsworth)

A heady mixture of fact and fiction combined in a compelling story of the Jacobean fight for the throne of England. Manchester's involvement and the formation of the Manchester Regiment. Authentic illustrations.

ISBN 1 872226 29 9 £4.95

Hobson's Choice (the Novel)

(Harold Brighouse)

The humorous and classic moving story of Salford's favourite tale. Well worth re-discovering this enjoyable story. Illustrated edition. Not been available since 1917, never before in paperback.

ISBN 1 872226 36 1 £4.95

More Stories Of Old Lancashire

(Frank Hird)

We present another 80 stories in the same easy, readable style, very enjoyable, great. With special section for Preston Guild 1992.

ISBN 1 872226 26 4 £4.95

Stories & Tales Of Old Lancashire

(Frank Hird)

Over 70 fascinating tales told in a wonderful light-hearted fashion. Witches, seiges and superstitions, battles and characters all here.

ISBN 1 872226 21 3 £4.95

Poems & Songs Of Lancashire

(Edwin Waugh)

A wonderful quality reprint of a classic book by undoubtedly one of Lancashire's finest poets. First published 1859 faithfully reproduced. Easy and pleasant reading, a piece of history.

ISBN 1 872226 27 2 £4.95

The Best of Old Lancashire — Poetry & Verse

Published in 1866 as the very best of contemporary Lancashire writing, this book now offers a wonderful insight into the cream of Lancashire literature in the middle of the last century. Nearly 150 years later, edited and republished, the book now presents a unique opportunity to read again the masters of our past.

ISBN 1 872226 50 7 £4.95

The Dock Road

(J. Francis Hall RN)

A seafaring tale of old Liverpool. Set in the 1860s, with the American Civil War raging and the cotton famine gripping Lancashire. Period illustrations.

ISBN 1 872226 37 X £4.95

The Lancashire Witches

(W. Harrison Ainsworth)

A beautifully illustrated edition of the most famous romance of the supernatural.

ISBN 1 872226 55 8 £4.95

Stories Of Great Lancastrians

(written Frank Hird)

The lives of 24 great men of the county, told in easy reading style. Complete with sketches and drawings, a good introduction to the famous of Lancashire and Manchester. John Byrom, Arkwright, Tim Bobbins, Duke of Bridgewater.

ISBN 1 872226 23 X £4.95

SONGS of a
LANCASHIRE WARBLER
Lowell Dobbs

The History of
Lancashire Cookery
PP
Tom Bridge

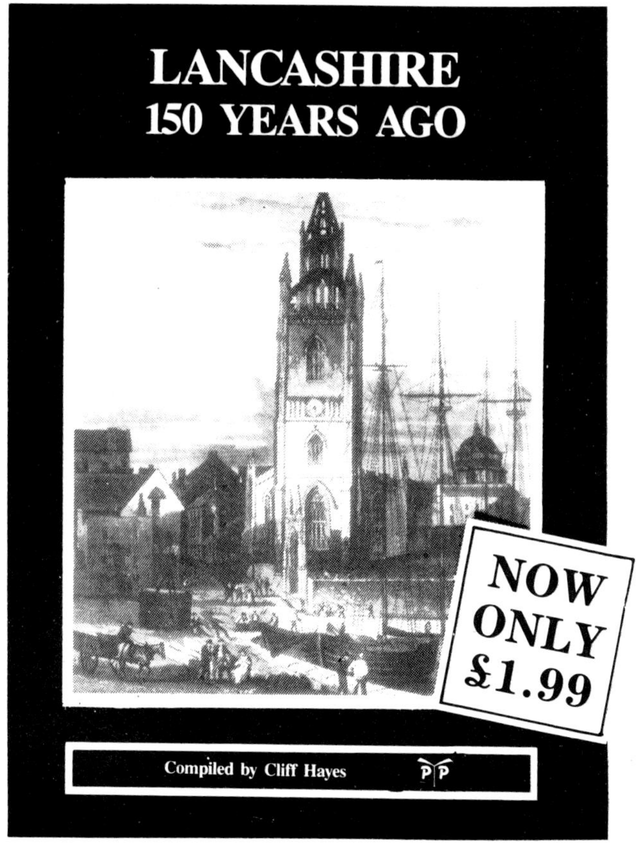
LANCASHIRE
150 YEARS AGO
NOW
ONLY
£1.99
Compiled by Cliff Hayes
PP